School Smarts
PROJECTS

Create TONS of great presentations, BOOST your creativity, IMPROVE your grades, and SAVE time and trouble!

By Dottie Raymer
Illustrated by Tracy McGuinness

★ American Girl™

Published by Pleasant Company Publications

Copyright © 2005 by American Girl, LLC

Questions or comments? Call 1-800-845-0005,
visit our Web site at **americangirl.com**, or write to
Customer Service, American Girl, 8400 Fairway Place, Middleton, WI 53562-0497.

Printed in China
07 08 09 10 C&C 10 9 8 7 6 5

American Girl™ and its associated logos are trademarks of American Girl, LLC.

Editorial Development: Sara Hunt, Michelle Watkins

Art Direction and Design: Camela Decaire, Chris David

Production: Kendra Schluter, Mindy Rappe, Jeannette Bailey, Judith Lary

Photography: Jamie Young, Sandy May

Cataloging-in-Publication Data available from Library of Congress

Special thanks to Maddie P., WI, for the science presentation on page 86.

Dear Reader,

Does the thought of a big project send shivers down your spine? Do you worry about getting all that work done on time, or wonder where to even begin? This book has all the secrets you need to tackle any big project. Get ideas for projects that you're sure to love doing. Get tips on how to stay on schedule. Find out the top five teachers' secrets for a no-fail report. And learn from the experts—girls just like you—how to make group work actually work. Big projects don't have to be scary. They're a chance to do what you do best— shine!

Your friends at American Girl

Contents

Tired of doing your reports by the book?

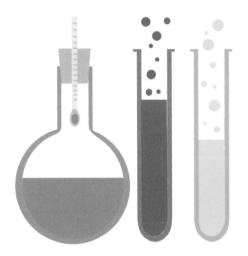

Are You a Procrastinator*?

Do you dillydally or dive right in? Pick the answer that describes you best.

1. Your mom just asked you to clean up your room. You . . .
   - a. shout, "Sure, Mom-as soon as this show is over."
   - b. declare, "It's my room! I like it the way it is!"
   - c. moan, "This will take forever! I'll be up all night!"
   - d. think, "Well, it does sort of look like a tornado hit it. I'll pick up the dirty clothes. Maybe that will help."

2. Your piano recital is on Saturday. Today is Monday. You . . .
   - a. ask your piano teacher if you can leave early to get to your soccer game.
   - b. tell yourself you'll do some extra practicing on Saturday morning.
   - c. wonder if it's too late to change to an easier piece.
   - d. block out 30 minutes for practice each day this week.

*Someone who puts off doing something.

6

3. It's 10 p.m. the night before your book report is due. You . . .
   a. ask your dad to write an excuse. It's not your fault your brother's band concert was tonight.
   b. figure you work best under pressure. Who needs sleep?
   c. crumple up your paper and throw it across the room. You'll never get it right!
   d. go to sleep. Your report is in your backpack and ready to go.

4. Your grandmother sent you a check for your birthday. You . . .
   a. plan to write the thank-you note after you spend the money. That way you can tell her what you bought.
   b. would write her if only you had some of those cute note cards you saw in the Girls' Stuff catalog.
   c. write "Dear Gran" and then put the note aside. You'll get back to it when you can think of something good to say.
   d. write a note telling her all the ways you're thinking of spending the money.

5. Your teacher passes out the assignment for your science project. You . . .
   a. slip the assignment into your science notebook. You can deal with this after the class play is over.
   b. shove the assignment into your backpack and forget about it. No need to worry—you're great in science.
   c. feel a knot in your stomach. What was that word? Hypothe-what?
   d. jot down the deadline in your assignment notebook.

Procrastinator Indicator

Mostly a's
Busy Lizzy

You're the girl who wants to do everything. You feel at your best when you have a lot going on. Sometimes, however, all that activity gets in the way of getting important things done. Try making a list of everything you need to do. Highlight what's most important, and do that first. Be realistic about how much you can take on at once. If soccer and karate both meet on Saturday mornings, tell yourself, "I can do only one thing at a time. Right now soccer is most important. I'll save karate for after soccer season is over."

Mostly b's
Last-Minute Lindsey

You're confident and want to do things your own way. You like the excitement of taking risks, and say that you work best under pressure. Unfortunately, you sometimes underestimate the time it will take to do an assignment, and then you end up handing in work that's late or less than your best. Look for other ways to show your confidence and smarts—maybe by picking a topic that really excites you or by creating a unique presentation. If you're excited by what you're doing, the time it takes to do it right will seem like fun.

Mostly c's
Nervous Nelly

You might feel overwhelmed by a big project and not know where to start. Or you might worry that even your best isn't good enough and try to do more than you need to do. Ask your teacher to go over the assignment with you so that you're sure about what you have to do. Remember, your teacher doesn't expect perfection—just good effort.

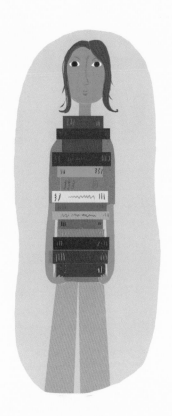

Mostly d's
Cool Hand Lucy

You like an easygoing pace and give your-self plenty of time to get things done. You know that this takes organization, and so you plan ahead. When you get the urge to procrastinate, you remember your motto for success: "Don't put off until tomorrow what you can do today!"

2, 4, 6, 8,
We Do NOT

Everyone needs a little motivation now and then.
Try one of these procrastination busters.

Try a baby step. Tell yourself, "All I need to do today is list some ideas for my report."

Take a 15-minute plunge. Set a timer for 15 minutes and work for all that time without stopping. The next day, try working for another 15 minutes. Soon you'll have it done!

Give yourself a reward. I made a little box and put in pieces of paper with rewards for certain amounts of work, such as a piece of gum for an hour's work. I liked the rewards so much that after a while, I just got into the habit of doing my work on time.

Start with the tough stuff. The trick is doing the hard stuff first and then the fun stuff. So, if you need to do an art project and a math paper, do the math paper and you will want to get to the art.

Procrastinate!

Write yourself a note. I write reminders on Post-it® notes and put them where I can see them. It really works!

Grab your attention. I got mirror markers from an art-supply store. Now whenever I have a project due, I write it and the due date on my mirror in green marker. That way I'll notice it each morning.

Make a deal. Make a pact with a study buddy to work on your papers for 10 minutes tonight.

Give yourself a pep talk. Think about another time when you worried but came out on top. Tell yourself, "I did it then. I can do it now!"

Talk it up. If facing a blank page is overwhelming, try talking through your ideas with a teacher or parent. As you talk, your thoughts will become more focused, and the whole project may begin to look more manageable.

BIG Truth.

There is a formula for success for every project.

1. Make a plan.
2. Investigate.
3. Arrange your information.
4. Put it all together.
5. Show it off.

Research Reports:
Getting Started

How to Read Teacher-ese

Assignments can be confusing—especially if they have lots of different directions. Read through your assignment carefully and highlight the important information. Ask yourself questions like these to make sure you understand exactly what the teacher wants.

Final Product

This is what your teacher wants to have in her hand when you're done.

What the Teacher Wants

Look for words that answer these questions:

- How long should the report be?
- What information should I include?
- What should it look like?

Colonial America Project

Choose a topic from the list on the board.

Your assignment is to make a scrapbook based on the information you gather about your topic.

Each scrapbook should include:

- A 1-2 page written report.

Examples

Pay close attention to the examples your teacher gives, but don't just use those examples. Be creative!

Due Date

Some teachers may put in separate dates for different parts of the project. If you're confused, ask!

- At least 2 pages of illustrations or photographs showing important events or objects related to your topic. For example, if you are researching colonial food, you might include copies of recipes or pictures of special cooking utensils the colonists used.

Your project is due on Wednesday, March 24.

Make a Date

Now that you know what to do, you need to figure out when to do it. It's time to get out the calendar!

Take It Apart
Break the assignment into smaller pieces.

Last Things First
Mark your due date on the calendar. Then work backward to set dates for each step of the project.

Guess-timate Your Time
How long will it take to choose a topic? Find your information? Write two paragraphs? Be honest with yourself about how long you think each step will take. Then make your best guess.

No Double-booking
Don't forget other activities, like basketball practice and piano lessons—and dinner! You can't take notes and eat tacos at the same time!

Expect the Unexpected
Try to leave a little extra time at the end, just in case you get the flu, or your computer crashes, or your dog . . . well, just in case!

Pencil It In
If something comes up and you get off schedule, don't panic. Just move your deadlines to fit the time you have left. That's what erasers are for!

MARCH

Sunday	Monday	Tuesday	Wednesday	Thursday	Friday	Saturday
	1 Piano 3:30	**2** Choose topic	**3** Basketball 4:00 Gather resources	**4** Start taking notes	**5** Basketball 4:00	**6** Get paper for scrapbook
7	**8** Piano 3:30	**9** Start writing report	**10** Basketball 4:00	**11**	**12** Basketball 4:00 Chorus Concert 7pm	**13** Gather pictures
14	**15** Piano 3:30 Finish writing report	**16** Draw or copy pictures for scrapbook	**17** Basketball 4:00	**18** Finish scrapbook. DON"T FORGET CAPTIONS	**19** Basketball 4:00	**20** Ask mom to proofread report
21 Finish up!	**22** Piano 3:30	**23**	**24** Basketball 4:00 Colonial project due	**25**	**26** Basketball 4:00	**27**
28	**29** Piano 3:30	**30**	**31** Basketball 4:00			

Techno Tip
Check your computer software to see if it has a calendar program. Just be sure to print out a copy so that you have it with you whenever and wherever you need it.

What's the Big Idea?

Stuck for a good idea? Use the Goldilocks Rule: not too big, not too little, but just right! First, jot down anything that comes to mind about the topic.

Project: Colonial America

Revolutionary War

funny hats

cornbread

Paul Revere

Boston Tea Party

shoes with big buckles

long poufy skirts

Deborah Sampson

muskets

Declaration of Independence

Next, choose an idea that strikes your fancy. Ask yourself:

Revolutionary War

Too big?

long poufy skirts
Too little?

If your idea is too big, cut it into smaller parts. If it is too little, think of a larger category it belongs to.

colonial clothing
Just right!

Finally, turn your just-right idea into a question.

How were colonial girls' clothes different from ours?

Pssst!

Teachers don't want you to be confused.

Bottom line:
If you don't know what your teacher wants, ask!

Research Reports:
Taking Notes

Ask Questions

Now let your mind wander—and wonder—about your big idea. Keep asking questions, and jot down your thoughts so that you don't forget them.

A mind map is a diagram that shows your thoughts. You can draw one by connecting your thoughts with arrows.

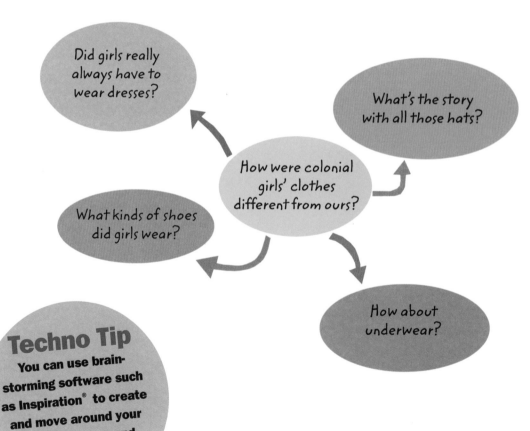

Did girls really always have to wear dresses?

What's the story with all those hats?

How were colonial girls' clothes different from ours?

What kinds of shoes did girls wear?

How about underwear?

Techno Tip

You can use brainstorming software such as Inspiration® to create and move around your own mind maps and diagrams on the computer.

Investigate

You have the questions. Now where do you find the answers? Tell everybody you know about your big idea. If they don't have the information you need, maybe they can point you in the right direction.

I remember reading a book called *If You Lived in Colonial Times* in fifth grade.

Your older sister

I know someone who works at the Historical Society. She might be able to help.

Your dad

I saw a great documentary called "A Revolutionary Girlhood" on television a while back. I wonder if it's out on DVD.

Your neighbor

Let's try looking under "colonial clothing" in the library catalog and see what we find.

Your librarian

Here is a list of Web sites with great information about colonial America.

Your teacher

My parents bought me a mob cap on our trip to Colonial Williamsburg last summer. Do you want to see it?

Your friend

Speedy Reading

Swoop

Flip through the book or scroll down through the Web site. Look at the pictures and diagrams. Read a paragraph or two. Does this book or Web site seem to have the information you need?

Scan

Read the first paragraph of a chapter or section to get a sense of what it's about. Look for words in bold or italic type, and read the sentences around them. If there are notes in the margins, read them first.

Skim

Check the table of contents. Read the titles and headings. Which chapters or sections are related to your topic?

Read

Look for the most useful information by paying close attention to words in fancy type or lists that are set off by bullets or numbers. If you come across a word you don't know, skip over it and read on. Its meaning will probably get clearer as you read. If you need to, jot down the word and look it up later.

Got a book? Got a Web site? Good. Now find your information. Luckily, you don't have to read every word . . . yet.

For Web sites

Use the FIND command in your EDIT menu to search for your topic or related words. Print out any information you want to read more carefully.

For Books

Check the book's index for words related to your topic to find additional information.

Flag It

Use self-sticking flags to mark important ideas or questions that come up. Make up a code that will remind you why you marked the spot.

!! Important idea

?? Huh? Don't get this.

Good details!

Web Tips

Have you ever tried an Internet search and found yourself caught in a tangle of Web pages? Here's how to avoid getting snagged.

Fine-Tune Your Keywords

Before you type a word, ask yourself, "How common is this word? How many different ways might people use it?" Limit your search by adding more specific words. Put the most important or precise words first.

Keywords: colonial times
Your search resulted in 186,000,000 pages.

Keywords: colonial children's clothes
Your search resulted in 57,000 pages.

Put a minus sign (-) in front of a word you don't want. If you want information on girls' clothes, not boys', type:

Keywords: colonial children's clothes -boys

Be a Critical Browser

How can you tell if a Web site is a good one? Keep "www" in mind:

Who is the author of this information? Is it clearly stated on the Web site?

What information are you getting? Is it clear and easy to understand?

Why do you want to use this information? Is it really related to your topic? If not, hit the Back button.

Quote a Phrase

Put a phrase in quotation marks to make sure the search engine sees it as one term.

Keywords: "colonial girls' clothes"

Safe Surfing

Follow your teachers' and parents' rules for using the Internet. Keep these two golden rules in mind:

 Never give out your full name, address, telephone number, age, birthday, or school to anyone over the Internet.

2 Sometimes a search will lead you to a site that makes you feel uncomfortable. Let your teacher or a parent know right away so that they can help you limit your search.

Take Note

How do you like to arrange things? Check the statements that sound most like you.

☐ I like finding interesting bits of information.

☐ I like to draw on my notes. ☐ I like to number my notes.

☐ I often erase or cross out notes so I can move them around. ☐ I like to plan things ahead of time so I don't have to make changes. ☐ I like to underline or circle information as I read it. ☐ I like to write down information as I read it. ☐ I arrange my notes with bullets or dashes.

☐ I like to highlight my notes in different colors. ☐ I usually draw a map when someone asks for directions.

☐ I give step-by-step directions to tell someone how to get somewhere. ☐ I'm constantly rearranging the furniture in my bedroom. ☐ Once I get my furniture the way I like it, I keep it that way for a long time.

☐ I usually look at the photos on the front page of a newspaper before anything else. ☐ I usually read the headlines on the front page of a newspaper before anything else.

TODAYS NEWS
FARMER SEES SPACESHIP LAND IN HIS FIELD

☐ I write notes to myself on my hand or on little pieces of paper to help me remember important things. ☐ I write everything I need to remember in an assignment notebook. ☐ I love bold, bright colors. ☐ I love soft, quiet colors. ☐ Drawing pictures helps me remember things. ☐ I like making up rhymes to help me remember things. ☐ I usually draw squiggles and curlicues when I doodle. ☐ I usually draw boxes and triangles when I doodle. ☐ I like to write plans for how I can reach my dreams. ☐ I just like to think about all the things I could do with my life.

Count how many you checked of each color, then turn the page for your note-taking style.

More Purples Than Oranges?

You're an orderly person who likes to make lists. Try using an outline to organize your notes.

Title · · · · · · · · · · · · · Girls' Fashions in Colonial Times

First paragraph · · · · · Introduction
· Girls dressed like their mothers.
· Different from today
· Example: corsets

Main idea of the paragraph

Underwear
· Stays (corsets)

Use bullets, dashes, · · · · · Hoops
or numbers to set off
different ideas. · Petticoats
· Separate pockets

Details · ·

Dresses
· Only one or two dresses
· Stomachers

Last paragraph

· Pattens

Conclusion
· Colonial fashions were fancy but uncomfortable.
· Today's clothes for girls are

More Oranges Than Purples?

You understand things best when you can see them as pictures in your head. Make a graphic organizer to put your notes in order.

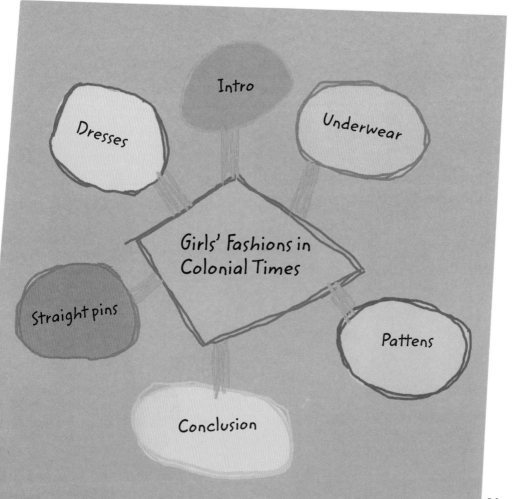

Intro

Dresses

Underwear

Girls' Fashions in Colonial Times

Straight pins

Pattens

Conclusion

Copycat . . .

Plagiarism (PLAY-juh-ri-zem): copying someone else's words or ideas and using them as your own

It's been said that imitation is the sincerest form of flattery. But there's a difference between gathering information and copying someone else's work.

To make sure you're copy smart, put quotation marks around any words you copy directly from a book, and give the source. Or get around the whole problem by jotting down only the important words in your notes. Then, when it comes time to write, you'll know your words are your own.

or Copy Smart?

If the original says . . .		Your paper should say . . .
If a corset was pulled too tight, it could cause dizziness. *(Welcome to Felicity's World)*		How would you feel *if* you had to wear a corset that was so tight, you could hardly breathe?
I have not been wet all over at once for 28 years past. *(The Diary of Elizabeth Drinker)*		One colonial woman wrote in her diary, "I have not been wet all over at once for 28 years past." That means she hadn't bathed in 28 years!
The word *dress* referred to formal clothing. *Undress* referred to everyday wear. (Dr. Lucinda Jacobs, *Colonial Times Magazine*, May 1998)		According to historian Lucinda Jacobs, even the words *dress* and *undress* had different meanings. Colonists called their formal clothes "dress." They called their casual clothes "undress."

BIG
Truth

**What's the most important thing to
keep track of as you research a topic?**

Your source, of course!

Research Reports:
Writing

Easy as . . .

Follow these three simple steps to writing a successful research report.

Remember that great movie you saw? You just had to tell your family all about it at the dinner table the next night.

Think of report writing in the same way. It really is just telling a story about what you know. And you're good at that, right?

1. Start by telling readers what you're going to tell them.

Remember your big idea? Start off with it. But make it worth listening to. Here are some ideas to grab your readers' attention:

- Ask a question: "How would you feel if you had to wear a corset all day?"
- Use a quotation: "'Dear Mama, You don't know the fashion here . . .' That's how one colonial girl began a letter to her mother."
- Give a hint about the strangest or most interesting fact you found: "Girls' corsets were so tight, girls could hardly breathe!"

Girls' Fashions in Colonial Times

How would you feel if you had to wear a corset that was laced so tightly, you could hardly breathe? Well, that's what colonial girls had to do all day long! Now girls have their own fashions and even their own stores. In colonial times, though, girls dressed just like their mothers—right down to corsets!

In colonial times, corsets were called "stays." They had long strips of wood in them to give you good posture. They also had laces that could be pulled tight to make a girl's waist look smaller. Some women pulled their corset

2. Back up your main idea with three examples or reasons.

This is where you tell what you've found out. But don't just chatter on, telling everything you know. Arrange your information into at least three sub–topics, with lots of details to back them up.

laces so tight that they broke their own ribs or fainted because they couldn't breathe. Corsets weren't the only underwear that girls had to wear. Many girls wore hoops around their hips to make their skirts look full. Over the hoops, they wore layers and layers of petticoats to keep warm. Dresses didn't have pockets, so girls tied separate pockets under their petticoats. Their money certainly would be safe there!

1st example

Colonial girls weren't allowed to wear pants. Usually, they had one or two everyday dresses and one dress for special occasions. Instead of buying a new dress, girls used "stomachers" to make their old dresses look different. Safety pins hadn't been invented yet, so girls used straight pins to pin stomachers and aprons right onto their dresses. Ouch!

2nd example

Colonists didn't take baths or wash their hair very often. So girls always kept their hair covered—even at night! During the day, they wore mob caps to keep smoke and dirt out of their hair. At night, they wore bonnets called "lappet caps" that tied under their chins. During the summer, they wore straw hats with wide brims—not to keep their hair clean, but to keep from getting freckles or a tan. They didn't have sunscreen then!

Shoes were very expensive, so girls usually had only one pair of everyday shoes and one pair of good shoes. Their everyday shoes were made of leather and had big heels and sometimes big buckles. Good shoes were often made of silk and decorated with embroidery and pearls. Only boys wore boots. If a girl wanted to keep her feet dry, she tied wooden platforms called "pattens" onto her shoes. Pattens were very hard to walk on, but at least they kept your feet out of the puddles.

Girls' fashions in colonial times were a lot fancier than they are today, but they were a lot less comfortable. As for me, I'll take a nice pair of comfy blue jeans any day!

3. Tell your readers what you told them.

Your conclusion is your chance to make sure your readers get your point. State your main idea again in a new way. End with a strong or snappy sentence that will make a lasting impression.

Time to Shine

What if you followed the formula and typed up your report—and it's still too short to hand in? Take a look at each part to see if something's still missing.

Beginning

- Have you stated your big idea? If not, write it down and put it in!
- Do you have a question, quotation, or interesting fact you can add?

Middle

- If you're reporting on a topic or book, can you compare or contrast the topic or the main character with your own life?
- If you're reporting on an event, are there any important details you've missed?
- Does every paragraph have a main idea? Can you find a few more facts to back up that idea?

End

- Have you added a paragraph that sums up what you think?
- Can you add a sentence or two to make your readers remember what you wrote?

Still Stalled?

Stimulate Your Senses

Splash your face with cold water. Bite into a crisp apple. Hum along with your favorite tunes. Waking up your senses will help wake up your brain.

Switch Gears

Get up and move around. Jump rope, shoot baskets, or even (yikes!) clean your room. Set a timer for 15 minutes so that you don't forget to get back to work.

Look for Inspiration

Flip through your book or reference materials again. Look at the pictures and jot down words that jump out at you.

Give It Drama

Close your eyes and imagine a movie or TV show about your topic. What do you see?

If you find yourself staring at a blank page, jump-start your creativity by looking at your topic from a different perspective.

Make Believe

Pretend you're a famous author speaking about your book, or a world-renowned scientist accepting an award for your research. What would you say?

Get It on Tape

Pretend you're a news reporter and record your ideas with a video recorder.

Draw It Out

Make a sketch of something you're writing about.

Let It Flow

For one or two minutes, write down every word or phrase that pops into your mind—whether or not it's related to your subject.

Whew! Finished!

Now it's time to put on your editor's cap. Read your report aloud to a friend or family member—or to yourself. Give your report a critical eye, from the top down.

Check Your Sentences

Does each sentence tell a whole thought? Do too many sentences begin the same way? Can you turn three similar sentences into one series? Or can you vary the sentence structure by reversing the order?

BLAH

Colonial girls wore corsets.
Colonial girls wore mob caps.
Colonial girls wore big-buckled shoes.

TAH-DAH

Colonial girls wore corsets, mob caps, and big-buckled shoes.

. . . Almost!

Check Your Meaning

Does the report make sense?
Have you stuck with your topic?
Is it upbeat and interesting?

Check Your Paragraphs

Does each paragraph have only one main idea? Do all the details support that idea? Each paragraph should have about four or five sentences.

Check Your Words

Do your words come alive on the page? Instead of writing, "The car went up the hill," try, "The old green car chugged up the steep hill."

Last, make sure your report is error-free!

Make a Great Impression

A well-researched, well-written report can be overlooked if it's not neatly organized or pleasantly presented.

Cover Story

Make a cover page for your report. Be sure your name, the date, and the name of the class are on the page. Illustrate with clip art or your own drawings. Remember, first impressions count!

If You Handwrite Your Report

- Some teachers like you to skip every other line on your notebook paper so they can write comments in between. Ask your teacher what she prefers.
- Use margins on both the left side (the red line) and the right side of the page. Don't run off the page!

Girls' Fashions

in

Colonial Times

Sara H.
March 24
Social Studies

in them to
ist look

If You Type Your Report

- **Use double-spacing and standard margins so that your sentences are easy to read.**
- **Print out your first draft and proofread it (or, better yet, ask someone else to read it, too).**
- **Make your changes on your computer. Then print out a clean copy.**

Letter-Perfect

You may be tempted to write in big loopy letters, use a giant type size, or spread out your words to take up space. Surprise! You're not fooling anyone. Pick an easy-to-read font, like Helvetica or Times New Roman, in 12-point type.

Last-Minute Changes

If you must cross something out in your final draft, don't scribble over it or erase a hole in the paper. Some teachers are OK with Wite-Out®. Others would rather you draw one line through a mistake and neatly print the correction over it. Make sure you know what's acceptable.

Don't Forget Your Source (of course!)

Include a bibliography so that everyone knows where you got your information. See the format at the back of the book to create your bibliography "by the book"!

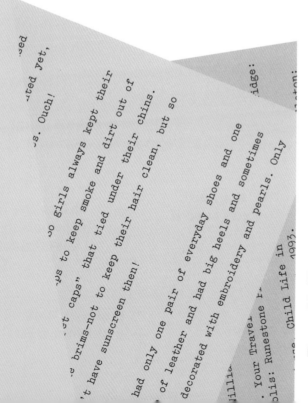

BIG Truth

We asked teachers what makes or breaks a great report or project. Here are their top answers:

It's neat. I can read it.

It has the information I asked for.

It's handed in on time.

It's in your own words.

It shows that you did your best.

Brilliant Book Reports

Got a Book?

Avid Annie

reads anything she can get her hands on. But now she has to choose a book for her report. How can she possibly choose?

Picky Paula

loves a good book—that is, if it's really good. How can she find a book she's sure she'll like?

Think about a subject that's recently caught your fancy or an issue important to you. Ask your librarian to suggest books that deal with that theme or topic.

Ask your best friend, mom, or favorite teacher to recommend one of her all-time favorite books. If someone you know has recommended a book you've liked in the past, chances are you'll like the next recommendation, too!

How do you find the perfect book for you? Knowing your reading style helps. Which reader below sounds like you?

Loyal Lilly

has read all 31 books in the Sleepover Sleuths series. What else might she like?

What is it that you love best about your favorite series? Solving the mysteries? Reading about characters who seem just like you? Once you know what grabs you, ask for other books or series that have the same appeal.

Magazine Maggie

has a stack of magazines a mile high by her bed. But books? Well, that's another story.

Look for collections of stories or books that are divided into short chapters or sections. If the articles you like are factual, ask your librarian or teacher to recommend nonfiction books on a similar subject.

Read It!

Once you find a book that excites you, make sure it's at the right reading level for you.

Thumbs Up?

Open the book in the middle and read a page.

- Hold up all five fingers (well, four and a thumb).
- As you read, put down one finger for each word you don't know or can't figure out.
- If you get to your thumb before you finish the page, the book might be too hard.

Now think again about the book. If you still really, really want to read it, try another page. Still seem too hard? Read it for fun when you don't have the time pressure of a book report.

Check a List

If your teacher has given you a list of books, start there—but don't stop there! For more ideas, ask your friends, parents, older siblings, classmates, and, of course, your librarian for a list of their favorites.

You might also look online or at your library for lists of books that have earned special recognition, such as a Newbery Medal or Parents' Choice award.

Don't forget to check out the lists of Surefire Books You're Bound to Love (and love reporting on!) at the back of this book.

Tap Your Interests

Make a list of some of your interests. Here are some possibilities:

• **Three things I do when I have spare time**

....

• **Three things I want to do when I'm older**

....

• **Three places I would go if I won a free trip anywhere**

....

• **Three things I've always wondered about**

....

Build a Better

Start your book report with the basic building blocks. Then add your own opinions—and back them up with examples from the book.

Who?
If you don't know who the main characters are, ask yourself these questions: "Who is telling the story? Who creates the problem in the story? Who solves it?"

When?
If the story doesn't happen in a specific time, tell what you imagined as you read. Is it present-day? Sometime in the future? What made you think that?

How?
Go back to the main problem. What is the one thing that happens that solves that problem?

What?
Most books have a climax, when you think to yourself, "Now what are they going to do?" That's where you'll probably find the problem.

Where?
If your book isn't set in a specific place, describe the details you remember about your main character's surroundings.

Why?
Remember, you're the critic. You don't have to like every book you read. If you loved the book, tell why. If you hated it, tell why. If you were lukewarm—you guessed it—tell why.

To Tell or Not to Tell?
Do you give away the ending or leave your readers guessing so that they'll read the book and find out for themselves? It depends on your assignment. If you're not sure, ask your teacher.

Book Report

Island of the Blue Dolphins
by Scott O'Dell

"I remember the day the Aleut ship came to our island." That is how Karana begins her story of Island of the Blue Dolphins. Karana is an American Indian girl who lives on an island in the Pacific Ocean during the 1800s. Island of the Blue Dolphins is the true-life story about how she is left alone on the island and learns to survive.

When the story begins, the Aleuts have just come to Karana's island to hunt otters. A fight starts between the hunters and the men from Karana's village, and most of the villagers are killed. Later, another ship arrives with "white men" who promise to take the remaining villagers to safety. Just when the ship is about to leave, Karana realizes that her little brother Ramo is not on board. She jumps overboard to rescue him, but it is too late. The ship leaves without them!

There are lots of scary and sad parts to this story, but there are happy parts, too. The best parts are when Karana makes friends with the dolphins, otters, and other wildlife. My favorite part of the book is when Karana saves Rantu, the leader of the wild dog pack, and nurses him back to health.

If you've ever wondered what you would do if you were left alone on a deserted island, then Island of the Blue Dolphins is the book for you!

The Un-Book Report

Tired of the same old style of book report?
Ask your teacher if you can try something different!

Interview the main character.

Write a diary from your favorite character's point of view.

Act out a scene with others who have read the book.

Create a slide presentation or Web site on the computer.

Make a board game based on the major events of the book.

FINISH

Give a speech while dressed up as one of the characters.

Make a scrapbook for one of the characters.

Draw a time line of the events of the book.

Write a newspaper article telling about the events.

Make a comic strip of the most important scene.

Create an infomercial— a TV commercial selling the book.

Design a book jacket.

Write a picture book for younger children based on the story.

Retell the story from a different character's point of view.

Collect or create several artifacts that are important in the story and tell why they're important.

Create a twenty-questions or trivia game about the book.

Write a poem or perform a song that tells the story.

Make a crossword puzzle using names or ideas from the book.

Make a mini book of the book.

Design a cereal box or other package based on something in the book.

Design a wanted poster for the main character.

Present a scene from the book as a radio show.

Make paper dolls or puppets of the main characters.

Write a letter from the main character's point of view.

Special Report

Put your report in a TV spotlight and dazzle your viewers . . . er, teacher!

Make a Show-in-a-Box

You will need:
- Shoe box • Paper roll • 2 dowels • Tape • Markers • Scissors

1. First decide how many scenes you'll need. Include an opening and a closing scene, if you like. Then measure a length of rolled paper that's long enough to accommodate all of your scenes, plus about 12 inches.

2. Have an adult cut a rectangle from the bottom of a shoe box, leaving about a 1-inch border. Save the center piece.

3. Make sure your paper roll fits into your shoe box. You may have to cut the paper to size. Then, with the curled side facing down, use the center piece from the shoe box as a template to make boxes for your scenes. Leave about an inch between scenes.

4. Hold the box so that you're facing the "screen." Have an adult poke holes at the top and bottom of both sides of the box, as shown.

5. Put the dowels through the holes. Then, from the back of the box, tape one end of the paper roll to one dowel. Your story should face "out."

6. Roll up the story onto one dowel and cut any excess paper. Tape the other end securely to the other dowel.

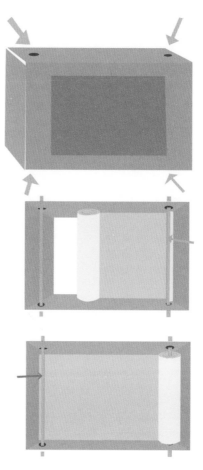

7. Wrap the box with foil. And you're ready to . . . roll!

ISLAND OF THE BLUE DOLPHINS

Q: My book report is due tomorrow, and I've only written the first paragraph! Help!

—Stuck

A: Believe it or not, even famous writers have moments when they can't think of another thing to say. Take a deep breath. Then look at your report with a fresh eye. Read your assignment out loud so that you hear every word. Think about what you need to include. Is there information you still haven't covered? Ask someone else to read what you've written so far and ask you questions about it. If you're still stuck, try skipping around. Write the ending of the report first, or jump right into the middle. Then go back and fill in the missing parts.

Projects

Project Smarts

How do you like doing things? Check the statements that describe you.

1. I'd rather draw a map than explain how to get somewhere.
   ☐ Yes, sounds like me. ☐ Nope, not usually.

2. I like to play card games and am good at them.
   ☐ Yes, sounds like me. ☐ Nope, not usually.

3. If I'm nervous, I talk a lot. *chatter chatter*
   ☐ Yes, sounds like me. ☐ Nope, not usually.

4. I pick up tunes I hear on the radio and hum them all day.
   ☐ Yes, sounds like me. ☐ Nope, not usually.

5. When I'm upset, I write in my diary.
   ☐ Yes, sounds like me. ☐ Nope, not usually.

6. If I have a good idea, I can get others to go along with it.
   ☐ Yes, sounds like me. ☐ Nope, not usually.

7. I like making or building things.
   ☐ Yes, sounds like me. ☐ Nope, not usually.

8. I like doing crossword puzzles and other word games.
   ☐ Yes, sounds like me. ☐ Nope, not usually.

9. I pick up new sports moves or dance steps quickly.
   ☐ Yes, sounds like me. ☐ Nope, not usually.

10. I like watching TV shows about groups of friends.
    ☐ Yes, sounds like me. ☐ Nope, not usually.

11. I like to hum, whistle, or sing in the shower.

☐ Yes, sounds like me. ☐ Nope, not usually.

12. I like competing as part of a team.

☐ Yes, sounds like me. ☐ Nope, not usually.

13. If I'm tense, I feel better if I move around.

☐ Yes, sounds like me. ☐ Nope, not usually.

14. I like seeing how things are put together.

☐ Yes, sounds like me. ☐ Nope, not usually.

15. If I'm upset, listening to music calms me down.

☐ Yes, sounds like me. ☐ Nope, not usually.

16. I like having quiet time when I can be by myself.

☐ Yes, sounds like me. ☐ Nope, not usually.

17. When spelling a word, I close my eyes and picture it.

☐ Yes, sounds like me. ☐ Nope, not usually.

18. I like to do math in my head more than on paper.

☐ Yes, sounds like me. ☐ Nope, not usually.

19. I like working with other people on projects.

☐ Yes, sounds like me. ☐ Nope, not usually.

20. I find it easy to remember friends' telephone numbers.

☐ Yes, sounds like me. ☐ Nope, not usually.

21. I'm very aware of my own and other people's moods.

☐ Yes, sounds like me. ☐ Nope, not usually.

Use Your Smarts

Count the number of symbols you checked YES. Then look below to see what kinds of projects might fit your style. Did you come up with a tie? That just means that you have lots of options!

Mostly Squares

You're tuned in to music and the sounds around you. Compose the sound track for a multimedia display. Create a song, jump-rope rhyme, or advertising jingle. Or better yet, perform it!

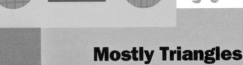

Mostly Triangles

You like words and use them well. Publish a newspaper or a brochure. Write letters or editorials. Make up crossword puzzles or word games. Give a speech or debate on your topic.

Mostly Flowers

For you, seeing is believing. Draw a diagram, a map, or a poster. Create a logo or a comic strip. Put together a photo album or collage.

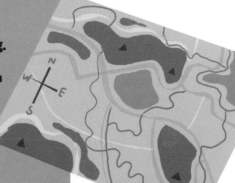

Mostly Circles

You like figuring out what makes you and other people tick. Write a diary or ship's log, or draw a family tree. Collect souvenirs for a scrapbook or travel journal.

Mostly Diamonds

You're a logical thinker. You're comfortable with numbers and like how they make sense. Set up charts or graphs to display your information. Construct number puzzles or quizzes. Use the computer to do your project.

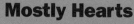

Mostly Hearts

You just want to move. Act out a scene or perform a skit. Cook a meal or demonstrate a science experiment. Choreograph a dance or pantomime performance.

Mostly Stars

You get along well with others and like working with a team. Conduct an interview or survey. Create a role-playing game or teach a lesson on your subject.

Reality Check

You've got the best-ever idea for a project! Can you pull it off? Ask yourself these three questions:

1. Do I have enough time to do what I want to do?

2. Do I know how to do it?

3. Do I have the materials? How much will they cost?

OCTOBER

1. Time

Building a model of the Eiffel Tower is a great idea! But can you do it in the time you have?

Tip: Think about your last project. How long did it take? Mark the due date on your calendar and count backward. Do you have enough time?

2. Trouble

Do you know how to do this? If not, who's going to help you?

Tip: Mom and Dad can figure out a lot of things, but it's not their job to figure out how to do your project. Try out your idea on a mini model. Did it work? If not, do you need to change your plan?

3. Money

List the materials you think you'll need. How many do you already have? How many will you need to buy?

Tip: Building your Eiffel Tower out of Legos® might be very cool, but only if you happen to have tons of Legos on hand. Look around your house for materials that you could use instead. Toothpicks? Twigs? Cardboard boxes?

Be Prepared

Keep supplies handy at home. You won't have to run out for materials at the last minute.

Colored pencils
Poster board (you know you'll need it—why wait?)
Hole punch
Permanent markers, fine and ultra-fine
Crayons
Colored markers
Highlighter
Scissors
12-inch ruler (with metric)
Wide-ruled notebook paper
No. 2 pencils
Eraser
Pencil sharpener
Post-it notes
Wite-Out
Glue
Stapler
Paper clips
Dictionary
Ribbon and fabric scraps
Scrapbook paper
Paper punches
Stickers
Alphabet stickers or stencils

Professional Art Quality

G'day Mate!

DANGER

AUSTRALIA

Dry

MID-NIGHT BLUE

The Great Display

Masai Mask
by Kate E.

The Masai people live in Kenya and Tanzania in East Africa. This mask was carved out of wood and worn by a warrior when he went into battle. Boys were given these masks during a special ceremony when they were 12 or 13.

Sources:
The Art of African Masks by Carol Finley
Joshua's Masai Mask by Dakari Hru

Facts First

Do research to find out exactly what your project should look like. Write a card or make a poster giving details about your display.

Give Credit Where It's Due

Include your own name and the name of the project on the card or poster. List any sources you used in your research.

The Right Stuff

Brainstorm a list of materials you could use to make your project. See what you have and what you need.

Be Careful

Take the time to do a thorough and neat job. Draw your design faintly in pencil so you know exactly where to paint. Let paint and glue dry completely before moving on to the next step. Whenever possible, use bright colors that catch the eye. Remember, though, that facts come first. A light blue polka-dotted mask may be pretty, but you won't get much credit for accuracy.

Transport Plan

How are you going to get your project to school? Your Masai mask won't look so great if it gets squashed on the school bus.

Media Mania

Tired of posters and display boards? Why not make a computer slide show? Or design a Web page? Or create a digital movie?

Check Your Resources

You'll need a computer, of course, and the right software program. If you want to take photos or make a movie, you'll also need a digital camera. Ask your school librarian or computer resource teacher for help in finding the equipment you need.

Find an Advisor

Who are you going to call if you run into technical difficulties? Ask a teacher, parent, older sibling, or techno-wiz friend if he or she will be available . . . just in case.

Sketch It Out

Map out what will be on each slide, Web page, or film clip. For example, if you're making a Web page, you'll want to plan where on the page you'll put your graphics, how much text you want to include, and how you want to set up your links.

Think Like a Graphic Designer

Do keep it simple.

Do use an easy-to-read font like Arial or Helvetica.

Do make sure the type color stands out from the background.

Do add borders and graphics after you put in the text.

Don't cram a lot of text onto one page.

Don't add too many graphics (even if they're cute).

Don't use too much animation. It gets annoying fast!

Do a Trial Run

Do a run-through to make sure there are no technical problems. Then do another one with the equipment you'll be using for the actual presentation.

Final Checks

Check for spelling, punctuation, and grammar errors. Smooth out any rough transitions with fade-ins or music.

Last-Minute

You read the assignment. You planned ahead. You started early. But it's 6 p.m. the night before the project is due, and it's still not done. Now what?

Look at the big picture.
Do you need to skip choir practice tonight? How about your math homework? Can that wait until tomorrow?

Make a plan.
How much do you have left to do? The most important thing to do now is to get to work!

Take a fresh look at your project.
Have you taken on too much? Instead of making three posters, maybe you can make one.

Take a deep breath.
Panicking has a way of freezing the brain, and you need all the brainpower you can get!

Don't give up.
Keep doing your best. Most teachers will give you at least partial credit for late work.

Meltdown?

Go to sleep.

It's hard to think clearly—or do good work—when you're exhausted. Tomorrow, when you're rested, you can take stock of the situation and come up with a plan if you're still not finished.

Don't make excuses.

Do tell your teacher where you stand.

She'll appreciate your honesty, even if she's disappointed with the results. Together you can come up with a plan for getting the work finished.

Role Call

Group projects go more smoothly when everyone has a job that she likes to do.

I'm good at organizing. I'll schedule our meetings and keep track of our progress.

Manager

I like reading and discovering new information. I'll find the reference materials we need and check our facts.

Researcher

I like to write, and I'm pretty good at typing. I'll keep a record of our ideas and type up the final paper.

Reporter

I like to draw and have a good eye for how things should look. I'll design the poster and draw the diagrams.

I'm a born ham and love the spotlight. I'll give the oral presentation.

Presenter

Designer

I pay close attention to details. I'll proofread the final draft and make sure everything's in order.

I know where to get the stuff we need. I'll collect the materials and return them when we're finished.

Editor

Materials Manager

Teamwork Troubles

"That's a dumb idea!"

Remember that you can disagree without being disagreeable. Say something positive about the idea before you criticize it. If one person in the group seems to be taking too much heat, step in and say, "Look, we're just brainstorming here. We need all the ideas we can get."

"Nobody's listening to each other!"

It's hard to hear anyone when everybody's talking at once. Try this method from a Native American tradition. Pass a "talking stick" (or pencil or pen) from person to person. Only the person with the stick should be talking.

"Nobody's listening to me!"

If you feel like one or two people are dominating the conversation, suggest that you each write down your ideas on a sheet of paper and read them aloud. Then put each idea to a group vote.

"This is boooring!"

Don't just sit there and grumble. You're part of this group, too! Think of ways you can use your own talents or ideas to add some pizzazz to the project.

"She's so bossy!"

At the beginning of the project, write down each person's job (use pages 76–77 as a guide). Then, if someone starts stepping on toes, you can nicely remind her who's doing what.

"Nobody's doing any work!"

Make sure each group member knows exactly what she needs to do. Then make a schedule with regular check-in times. If it seems like someone's slacking off, help her brainstorm ways to get back on track.

"We can't agree on anything!"

If you just can't come to a decision, put it to a vote. Or write the top three choices on slips of paper and draw one out of a hat.

Q: I have to do a group project with this really annoying kid. He bugs me and loses points for our group. He doesn't do his work, and the teachers don't even notice. Our groups don't get switched for six weeks! What can I do?
—Group Troubles

A: Having to work with difficult people is a fact of life, but that doesn't make it any easier. It could be that Mr. Difficult doesn't think the rest of the group is interested in what he has to offer. The next time you have a project assigned, make it a point to involve him from the very beginning. Ask his opinions when you're brainstorming ideas, and really try to listen to what he has to say. List the jobs that need to get done, and give him his choice. Set up regular review times to check that he—and everybody else—is staying on track. If he still slacks off, ask for a group meeting with your teacher. Do this well before the project is due so that, if necessary, you can reassign jobs to get the project done.

Science Fairs with Flair

I Wonder...

Looking for a great science fair idea? Start with your own curiosity. Fill in the blanks with subjects you've always wondered about.

1. How does .... work?
   (subject)

(How does a gel pen work?)

2. What would happen if I ....
   (action)

.... to .... ?
   (subject)   (different subject)

(What would happen if I added extra baking soda to a recipe?)

3. What is the effect of ....on
   (subject)

.... ?
   (different subject)

(What is the effect of rap music on my dog's appetite?)

4. Which .... does .... best?
   (subject)   (action)

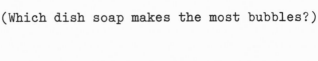

(Which dish soap makes the most bubbles?)

5. How is a .... different from

(subject)

a.. ?

(different subject)

(How is Bargain Brand X different from Famous Brand Y?)

6. How can I build a better... ?

(subject)

(How can I build a better alarm clock?)

7. Does...really ....

(subject)   (action)

.... ?

(more action)

(Does my cat really hear sounds I can't hear?)

8. What is the best way to...

(action)

....?

(subject)

(What is the best way to get rid of ants?)

Everyday Science

Still uninspired? Try one of these.

Newspapers & Magazines

What headlines grab your attention? An earthquake in Japan? An oil spill in Alaska? A new fossil discovered in North Africa? Can you turn your interest into a project?

Read the Label

Can you believe everything you read on the label of a can of soup or a bottle of shampoo? Just what does all that information on your cereal box tell you? What doesn't it tell you?

Advertisements

Do those sneakers really make you run faster and jump higher? Does one toothpaste really get your teeth whiter than another? How can you prove or disprove their claims?

Kitchen Science

Cooking involves all kinds of chemical reactions. Experiment with different amounts of key ingredients, like baking soda or vegetable oil, in your favorite recipes to put your taste buds to the test!

Fact or Fiction?

Is it true that carrots make you see better? Or does your dad tell you that just to make you eat your vegetables? How can you find out?

Web Idea

The Internet is a great place to look for science-fair project ideas. Try one of these sites for starters:

all-science-fair-projects.com
school.discovery.com/sciencefaircentral
scifair.org

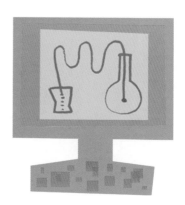

Fair Finesse

Present your findings with a flourish.

DATA

Name	Resting Heart Rate	Backstroke Heart Rate	Freestyle Heart Rate	Butterfly Heart Rate
Katie	88	148	160	198
Jenny	88	136	142	196
Olivia	100	140	148	176
Maddie	108	180	180	196
Allie	128	156	158	184
Average	102	152	157	190

SCIENTIFIC SWIMMING

HYPOTHESIS

Q: Which swimming stroke brings your heart rate up the most—backstroke, freestyle, butterfly?

A: I believe butterfly will bring the heart rate up the most because butterfly makes me the most tired of any stroke.

VARIABLES

1. Manipulated Variable: the stroke type
2. Responding Variable: the heart rates of the swimmers
3. Constant Variables: 25-meter pool, heart rate monitors

PROBLEM

When the girls dove into the water, the Polar heart rate monitor watches filled up with water and would not show a heart rate. So we took each girl's heart rate by watching the clock and counting her heartbeats per minute.

RESULTS

My results were expected. Butterfly brought the girls' heart rates up the most. The difference between their resting heart rates and butterfly heart rates was about 88 beats. The butterfly average heart rate was 190, the freestyle rate was 157, and the backstroke rate was 152.

CONCLUSION

I did get the results I expected. I knew butterfly would make people most tired because it makes me the most tired. I didn't expect the heart rate monitors to fill with water because they were supposed to be waterproof. But all in all, I think I still collected accurate data.

Backstroke
Freestyle
Butterfly

Scientific Swimming

Make your project easy to understand.

Use a tri-fold board for your display. Most office-supply stores carry display boards in different colors. Be sure everything on the poster is clearly labeled.

Follow your teacher's instructions about what to put in your report.

Most reports include:

- **Introduction** State the purpose of your experiment and your hypothesis.
- **Description** List the materials you used and the steps of the experiment.
- **Evidence** Keep track of what happened when on a calendar or in a journal.
- **Charts and graphs** Tally your information in a chart or graph. Then copy it to show on your display board.
- **Conclusion** What did you find out? It doesn't matter if your hypothesis was right or wrong. Remember, everyone likes a surprise ending!
- **Credits** List where you got your information. Don't forget to give credit to Mom, Dad, or anyone else who helped!

DO

give your display a catchy title in big, bold letters.

type or print your information in your neatest handwriting.

place your printed material on colorful
squares of construction paper.

lay everything out on your display board before you glue.
Use a glue stick rather than white glue to
attach charts and papers. It's neater.

use photos or models of your results or show how you got them.

decorate your display board.
Choose two or three colors that complement each other.

read over your work one more time to catch any
last-minute mistakes.

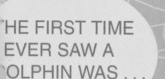

THE FIRST TIME
EVER SAW A
DOLPHIN WAS . . .

My favorite movie of all time was directed by . . .

Good morning!
Today I'm going
to talk about . . .

Oral Reports

The giant redwood tree
can be found in...

I FIRST BECAME INTERESTED
IN HORSES WHEN I WAS 4 YEARS OLD...

BONJOUR!

Hello, everybody.
I'm here to tell you about
the world of frogs . . .

Star Performance

Is there an oral report in your future? Think like a pop star! The secret to any great performance is…

Preparation

A good concert starts with a song list. A good presentation starts with information. Make sure you've got the facts. Then put them in an order that's easy for both you and your audience to follow. Try opening with a joke or a quote to catch your audience's attention.

Practice

Practice your report in front of your mom, your best friend, your cat—anyone who will listen. The more you practice, the more chances you have to work out any kinks and the more smoothly the words will flow when it's showtime.

HAWAii

Pizzazz

Don't be afraid to add a little drama. Bring in props and use posters or a slide show to set the scene. Dress in costume and ham it up. Now, that's entertainment!

Cures for the Jitters

Got butterflies? Here's advice for calming your nerves.

TICK TOCK!

Try to focus your attention on something at the back of the room and keep looking at that. That way, you don't have to look at all the people.
—Emily

Read your information to yourself over and over again. The better you know the information, the easier it will be to improvise if you get stuck.
—An American Girl

Whenever I get on a stage, I pretend there is no one in the audience. When that doesn't work, I pretend everyone in the audience is wearing something really funny. Remember to hold in your giggles, though!
—Elizabeth

Remember that the audience doesn't know what your report says, so they won't know if you mess up!
—Tiffany

Try picking one person in the room, like a friend or a teacher. Then pretend that you're presenting only to that one person.
—Eilidh

Try to practice in front of a mirror first, so you get used to talking to yourself. Then try it in front of your siblings or parents. If that's too embarrassing, try practicing in front of your stuffed animals!
—Allie and Leilani

Have fun! If you have fun while you're doing it, other people will have fun watching you.
—An American Girl

Always remember, everyone makes mistakes. If you make a mistake while in the spotlight, don't make a big deal out of it because some people may not have even noticed it! Also, in the long run, people usually remember a person's strong point, not her mistakes.
—Claire

BIG Truth

Projects give you a chance to

- show who you are and what you can do
- try something you've never done before
- make yourself proud!

A project is your chance to shine.

Have you made
a great school
presentation?
How about a shining
school project
or book report?

Tell us about it!

Write to:

School Smarts Editor
American Girl
8400 Fairway Place
Middleton, WI 53562

Here are some other American Girl books you might like:

❑ I read it.

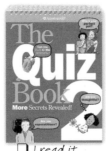

❑ I read it.

❑ I read it.

❑ I read it.

❑ I read it.

❑ I read it.

Surefire Books You're Bound to Love!
(and love reporting on)

Fiction

Because of Winn-Dixie
by Kate DiCamillo

Heartbeat
by Sharon Creech

*Nothing's Fair
in Fifth Grade*
by Barthe DeClements

P.S. Longer Letter Later
by Paula Danziger and
Ann M. Martin

Queen of the Sixth Grade
by Ilene Cooper

*What Every Girl
(Except Me) Knows*
by Nora Raleigh Baskin

Fantasy

Ella Enchanted
by Gail Carson Levine

*The Last of the Really
Great Whangdoodles*
by Julie Andrews

Lucinda's Secret
by Holly Black

Song of the Wanderer
by Bruce Coville

A Wrinkle in Time
by Madeleine L'Engle

Mysteries

The Egypt Game
by Zilpha Keatley Snyder

*From the Mixed-Up Files
of Mrs. Basil E.
Frankweiler*
by E. L. Konigsburg

Holes
by Louis Sachar

*Sammy Keyes
and the Hotel Thief*
by Wendelin Van Draanen

The Westing Game
by Ellen Raskin

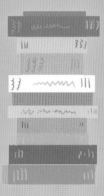

Nonfiction

*Brain Surgery for
Beginners and Other
Major Operations for
Minors: A Scalpel-Free
Guide to Your Insides*
by Steve Parker

*Fire in Their Eyes:
Wildfires and the
People Who Fight Them*
by Karen Magnuson Beil

*Go for the Goal:
A Champion's Guide
to Winning in Soccer
and Life*
by Mia Hamm

Kids on Strike!
by Susan
Campbell Bartoletti

*Lost Star: The Story
of Amelia Earhart*
by Patricia Lauber

Tear out these bookmarks for handy reference. The next time you need to pick a great book, you'll have several to choose from!

Biography

Cleopatra
by Diane Stanley

*Eleanor Roosevelt:
A Life of Discovery*
by Russell Freedman

*Light Shining Through
the Mist:
A Photobiography
of Dian Fossey*
by Tom L. Matthews

*Lives of the
Presidents: Fame,
Shame (and What the
Neighbors Thought)*
by Kathleen Krull

Through My Eyes
by Ruby Bridges

Historical Fiction

Bat 6
by Virginia Euwer Wolff

Catherine, Called Birdy
by Karen Cushman

A Long Way from Chicago
by Richard Peck

Number the Stars
by Lois Lowry

*The Watsons
Go to Birmingham*
by Christopher Paul Curtis

Animal Stories

Charlotte's Web
by E. B. White

*The Cricket in Times
Square*
by George Selden

The Secret of NIMH
by Robert C. O'Brien

*Island of the Blue
Dolphins*
by Scott O'Dell

Misty of Chincoteague
by Marguerite Henry